Take time to read and laugh every day !! :)

— Lisa Ayotte :)

"This is the day the that the Lord has made; let us rejoice and be glad in it."
(Psalm 118:28-29)

Thank you to my family & friends for your continuous encouragement & support!

"It is the sweet, simple things in life which are the real ones after all."
–Laura Ingalls Wilder

Some miniatures featured in this book were created by the following talented artists on Instagram: @adaliarose.dollhouseminiatures, @alymaesminis, @a_novel_mini, @bitsynest, @calico_garden, @cheries_mini, @cojiscrittercrafts, @etsy_karenbaby8, @fortheloveofsmallthings, @geniesminihouseshops, @kellylynminiatures, @lenniestinyworld, @littlestgiftshoppe, @magnolia_minis, @melvinsminiatures, @mforminiatures @mimi_miniature_boutique, @miniature_food_artist, @momosminicrafts, @mxdlcreations, @myminifrontporch, @mynewminihome, @mytinynestminiatures, @onesixthfauxlife, @petitegiteminiatures, @petiteprovisionsco, @shrewminiatures, @smallfunshop, @stylishlytiny, @sweetpeatoysminiatures @thedaintyhouse, @theminimeadow, @tiarastinykitchenhabit, @tinybitsyart, @wennysminis, @whiterabbitminis

Copyright © 2022 by Lisa Ayotte, Punny Peeps
All rights reserved. No part of this publication may be reproduced, distributed or transmitted in any form or by any means, including photocopying, recording, or other electronic or mechanical methods, without the prior written per-mission of the author.
Punnypeeps.com   Instagram: @punnypeeps1
Bristol, CT 06010
www.lisa@punnypeeps.com
Logo Design by Joe Philippon @ www.joephil.com
Photographs copyright ©by Lisa Ayotte, Punny Peeps
Punny Peeps' Fun Farm Jokes— First Edition©2022
ISBN 978-1-95127-816-8
Printed in the United States of America

PUNNY PEEPS' FUN FARM JOKES

LISA AYOTTE

PEEP 1: Where do sheep keep their school supplies?

PEEP 2: In their *baa-ckpacks!*

PEEP 1: What did the farmer do to stuff the turkey?

PEEP 2: He fed him A LOT!

PEEP 1: How do chickens stay in shape?

PEEP 2: They *eggs-ercise!*

PEEP 1: What is a lamb's favorite kind of pie?

PEEP 2: *Baa-nana* cream!

PEEP 1: What do ducks like to watch on TV?

PEEP 2: Duck-umentaries!

PEEP 1: What do horses like to drink in the summer?

PEEP 2: *Lemon-neighed!*

PEEP 1: What do cows like to drink in the summer?

PEEP 2: SMOO-thies!

PEEP 1: What do you get when a pig and chicken meet for breakfast?
PEEP 2: *Ham and eggs!*

PEEP 1: What do you call chickens in a hot tub?

PEEP 2: Soup!

PEEP 1: Why was the cow the best baker in town?

PEEP 2: Because he made the BIGGEST *pies!*

PEEP 1: Where does the farmer's wife like to shop?

PEEP 2: At the *Farmers* Market!

PEEP 1: What is a turkey's favorite dessert?

PEEP 2: Peach *gobbler!*

PEEP 1: What do sheep like to play in the summer?

PEEP 2: *Baaad-minton!*

PEEP 1: How do chickens make their desserts?

PEEP 2: From *scratch!*

PEEP 1: Why did the farmer put seeds in his pond?

PEEP 2: He wanted to grow some *water-melons!*

PEEP 1: Why can't you play hockey with pigs?

PEEP 2: They always *hog* the puck!

PEEP 1: What do ducks eat for lunch?

PEEP 2: Soup and *quackers!*

PEEP 1: Why did the farmer bring cookies to the horses?

PEEP 2: To welcome them to the *neigh-borhood!*

PEEP 1: How do you know carrots are good for your eyes?

PEEP 2: Because you *never* see rabbits wearing glasses!

PEEP 1: What do cows put on their sandwiches?

PEEP 2: Lots of *Moo-stard!*

PEEP 1: What is a sheep's favorite kind of car?

PEEP 2: A *Lamb-orghini!*

PEEP 1: Where did the horse go when he got hurt?

PEEP 2: To the *horse-pital!*

PEEP 1: What do you call a bull that does yoga?

PEEP 2: *Flexi-bull!*

PEEP 1: What do farmers say to plants to help them grow?

PEEP 2: "I *be-leaf* in you!"

PEEP 1: Where do cows like to go on vacation?

PEEP 2: *Moo York!*

PEEP 1: Why did the farmers bury their money?

PEEP 2: Because they wanted to make their soil *rich!*

PEEP 1: Why did the cows cross the street?

PEEP 2: To get to the *udder* side!

PEEP 1: Why couldn't the farmer stop eating leftovers?

PEEP 2: Because it's hard to *quit cold turkey!*

PEEP 1: Why did the goats get sent to the Principal?

PEEP 2: Because they kept *butting* heads!

PEEP 1: What did the farmer like best about school?

PEEP 2: The *field trips!*

PEEP 1: What is a scarecrow's favorite kind of ice cream?

PEEP 2: *Straw-berry!*

PEEP 1: What do rabbits like to eat for dessert?

PEEP 2: Carrot cake!

READING is PEEP-TASTIC!

We hope you had FUN, but now the Punny Peeps have to run! We're busy creating more *PUNNY* jokes and scenes for our next book! We believe sharing a good laugh with family and friends is the BEST! Laughter has the power to connect us to others, reduce stress, improve our mood, thus making us happier!

And we know you have LOTS of funny jokes that you LOVE to tell. SO...get out some paper and write them down! Next, create your characters and scenes to go along with them. Then, bind it together and you'll have a personalized joke book! You can also make some of your own SILLY Punny Peeps by gluing googly eyes onto colorful pom poms and adding details with scraps of paper or fabric. Be creative and have FUN!!

Until we see you again, always remember that it's the "little" things that matter most! YOU can change the world, one Peep at a time, by being a good friend and showing kindness to others each day!!! ☺